anythink

Sanitation Workers

By JoAnn Early Macken

Gareth Stevens
Publishing

Please visit our Web site, www.garethstevens.com. For a free color catalog of all our high-quality books, call toll free 1-800-542-2595 or fax 1-877-542-2596.

Library of Congress Cataloging-in-Publication Data

Macken, JoAnn Early, 1953-
 Sanitation workers / JoAnn Early Macken.
   p. cm. – (People in my community)
 Includes index.
 ISBN 978-1-4339-3810-8 (pbk.)
 ISBN 978-1-4339-3811-5 (6-pack)
 ISBN 978-1-4339-3809-2 (library binding)
 1. Street cleaners–Juvenile literature. 2. Street cleaning–Juvenile literature. I. Title.
 TD813.M33 2011
 628.4'4–dc22
                                    2010013210

New edition published 2011 by
Gareth Stevens Publishing
111 East 14th Street, Suite 349
New York, NY 10003

New text and images this edition copyright © 2011 Gareth Stevens Publishing

Original edition published 2003 by Weekly Reader® Books
An imprint of Gareth Stevens Publishing
Original edition text and images copyright © 2003 Gareth Stevens Publishing

Art direction: Haley Harasymiw, Tammy Gruenwald
Page layout: Daniel Hosek, Katherine A. Goedheer
Editorial direction: Kerri O'Donnell, Diane Laska Swanke

Photo credits: Cover (sanitation worker), back cover (sanitation worker) p. 1 (sanitation worker) Mike Kemp/Getty Images; cover (sanitation truck), back cover (sanitation truck), p. 1 (sanitation truck) Comstock/Getty Images; pp. 5, 13, 17, 21 © Gregg Andersen; pp. 7, 15 Shutterstock.com; p. 9 Matt Cardy/Getty Images; p. 11 © iStockphoto.com; p. 19 AFP/Getty Images.

Printed in the United States of America

CPSIA compliance information: Batch #CS10GS: For further information contact Gareth Stevens, New York, New York at 1-800-542-2595.

Table of Contents

Boldface words appear in the glossary.

A Clean Community

Sanitation workers help keep a community clean. They pick up **garbage**. They pick up bottles and cans that will be made into new bottles and cans.

Doing Their Jobs

Sanitation workers must sometimes carry heavy garbage cans. They lift heavy bags into a truck.

Sanitation workers wear thick gloves. The gloves help workers hold on to things. They also guard workers' hands from sharp objects, dirt, and **germs**.

Sanitation workers ride in big trucks. They put the garbage, bottles, and cans in the trucks. They usually follow a different **route** each day of the week.

At the end of the day, sanitation workers make sure everything is out of the truck. The garbage goes to a **landfill** or is burned.

Sanitation workers sometimes drive huge **street sweepers**. Street sweepers clean up dirt, leaves, and trash. They spray water on the streets, too.

street sweeper

Sanitation workers help keep parks and other public places clean, too. They pick up garbage and litter.

Sanitation workers do their jobs in all kinds of weather. They may drive **snowplows** in winter to clean snow off streets.

snowplow

How Can You Help?

You can help keep your community clean. Don't litter. Remember to always throw your trash into a trash can.

trash can

Glossary

garbage: trash and waste

germ: something that causes illness

landfill: a place where garbage is buried under dirt

route: a path of travel

snowplow: a truck with a large blade to push snow aside

street sweeper: a large truck that sweeps and washes streets

For More Information

Books

Hock, Peggy. *Our Earth: Making Less Trash.* New York, NY: Children's Press, 2009.

Miller, Heather. *What Does a Sanitation Worker Do?* Berkeley Heights, NJ: Enslow Elementary, 2005.

Web Sites

Environmental Kids Club

www.epa.gov/kids
This site gives information about garbage and recycling as well as ideas for helping our environment.

Welcome to Recycle City

www.epa.gov/recyclecity/mainmap.htm
A computer-game site of activities with information about recycling.

Index

About the Author

JoAnn Early Macken is the author of children's poetry; two rhyming picture books, *Cats on Judy* and *Sing-Along Songs*; and various other nonfiction series. She teaches children to write poetry and received the Barbara Juster Esbensen 2000 Poetry Teaching Award. JoAnn is a graduate of the MFA in Writing for Children Program at Vermont College. She lives in Wisconsin with her husband and their two sons.